A CLOSER LOOK BOOK
Published in the United States by
Franklin Watts in 1976

Designed by David Cook and
Associates and produced by
The Archon Press Ltd,
28 Percy Street,
London W1P 9FF

The authors wish to
acknowledge the assistance
received from Mrs. Joyce Pope
of the British Museum (Natural
History), London, during the
preparation of this book.

First published in
Great Britain 1976 by
Hamish Hamilton
Children's Books Ltd,
90 Great Russell Street,
London WC1B 3PT

Printed in Great Britain by
W. S. Cowell Ltd,
Butter Market, Ipswich

Library of Congress
Catalog Card Number: 75–44810
ISBN (Library edition): 0–531–01190–9
ISBN (Trade edition): 0–531–02434–2

A closer LOOK at OCEAN LIFE

Susannah and David Cook

Illustrated by
Roy Coombs

Franklin Watts · New York · London · 1976

Realms of the sea

The watery planet

Oceans cover more than 70 percent of the earth's surface. Life first appeared in the oceans, and today the seas provide living space for many thousands of species. The seas, of course, have three dimensions of living space— depth as well as length and width.

People have traveled to the moon millions of miles away and have thoroughly explored the land where they live. However, they have only recently started to probe beneath the oceans covering over 70 percent of the earth's surface.

Underwater mountain ranges stretch for hundreds of miles, and chasms even deeper than the Grand Canyon are hidden in the depths. In the South Pacific the greatest peak on earth rises from the deep-sea floor, becoming Mount Mauna Kea on Hawaii.

But much of the ocean landscape is flat and featureless. The sea bed slopes gently away from the shoreline, sometimes for hundreds of miles. This is the continental shelf. Here 90 percent of sea life is found, either swimming freely or living on the sea bed itself. At the edge of this shelf the sea floor drops away to where the real ocean depths begin.

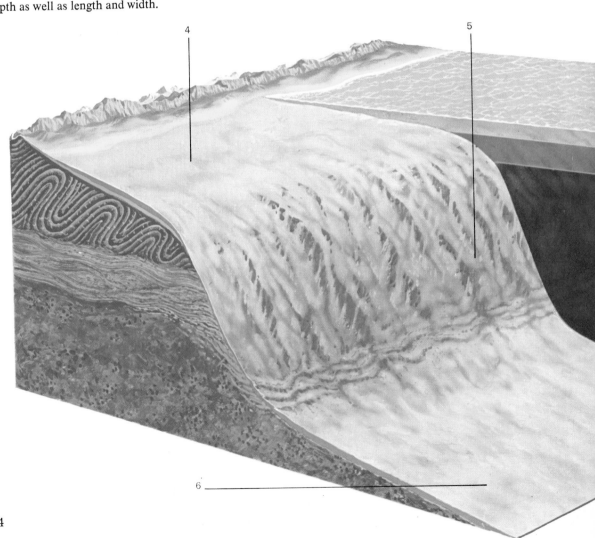

Because the density of sea water is 800 times as great as that of air, it was thought until the last century that life could not exist in really deep waters. But by using modern deep-sea equipment, divers have brought to the surface species that had once been thought extinct for millions of years. These "living fossils" prove that life can flourish even in the depths, where food is scarce, where the temperature never rises to more than a few degrees above freezing, and where the weight of the overhead water would crush any animal not specially adapted to living in such conditions.

In every part of the oceans there is a great variety of life. Sea birds skim the surface waters for food. Many species (kinds) of mammals and reptiles have chosen to return to the sea to live. Creatures ranging from those too small to be seen by the naked eye to the greatest animal ever to live on earth all depend on the resources of the vast ocean.

The ocean habitats

The ocean habitat can be divided into two main areas. The sea bottom and the plants and animals that live there make up the benthic division. The pelagic division is the name given to the open waters of the sea—the home of the drifters and the free swimmers. It can be divided in turn into three layers. The upper layer of the ocean (1) extends as far as 3,000 feet, but sunlight penetrates only the upper part of this layer, and the water temperature averages 50° F. It drops to about 40° F in the middle layer (2), which extends from 3,000 to 10,000 feet. The bottom layer (3), known as the abyss, extends to an average depth of 20,000 feet, although there are trenches up to 35,000 feet deep, and the water temperature is always below 40° F. In the benthic division the continental shelf (4) slopes gently out to sea, sometimes for hundreds of miles, to fall away to the continental slope (5). The continental slope continues down to the ocean floor (6), where the landscape consists of endless plains, mountain ranges, and trenches.

Ocean pastures

Land plants

Land plants are anchored to the ground. They absorb water and minerals through their roots and sunlight through their leaves.

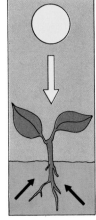

Sea plants

Most sea plants float freely. They absorb minerals from the waters that surround them and sunlight from above.

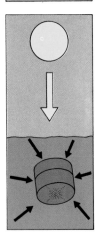

The surface of the sea is like a fertile meadow, with animals grazing on growing plants. Millions of microscopic plants are scattered like dust in the surface layers of the water.

These plants, with the tiny animals who feed on them, make up the layer called plankton—"that which drifts." The plants are phytoplankton and the animals zooplankton.

Phytoplankton can only live in the sunlit surface waters where they can absorb the sun's rays. They get all the nutrients they need from the surrounding waters. In temperate seas, when the sun is strong and there are plenty of nutrients, phytoplankton flourish, giving the water a green-gray tinge.

Zooplankton range in size from tiny forms no larger than a grain of rice to shrimplike animals called krill. They feed directly on phytoplankton, as well as sometimes on each other. They turn the vegetable matter into animal protein in a form that can be eaten by larger sea animals. Where the waters are rich in plankton, all the life of the sea flourishes.

The eggs and larvae of fish, crabs, mollusks, and many other organisms drift with the plankton layer until they are mature enough to fend for themselves.

Plankton

The smallest and most numerous members of the plankton are plants—the diatoms and dinoflagellates. Diatoms (1) are box-shaped one-celled organisms; they often hook onto each other to make chains of cells. Their cell walls are made of silica (a mineral). Holes allow sea water to enter the cells. This helps to keep them afloat. Dinoflagellates (2) are slightly larger. They propel themselves through the water with tiny whips (called flagella). These phytoplankton are eaten by small zooplankton, such as copepods (3), barnacle larvae (4), and crab larvae (5). Other than jellyfish, the largest members of the plankton are euphausiids (6), amphipods (7), squid larvae (8), arrowworms (9), and larval fish (10). Many of the larger zooplankton feed on fish eggs (11).

The key (right) refers to the illustration below. The phytoplankton are colored green; the zooplankton are colored gray if they are permanent or blue if they are temporary. Temporary members include the eggs and larvae of fish and shellfish.

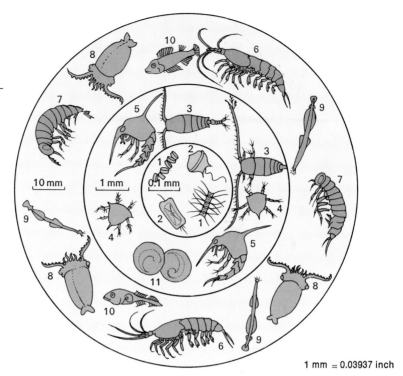

1 mm = 0.03937 inch

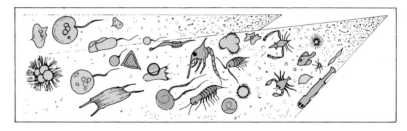

7

Eat and be eaten

Sea creatures spend most of their time searching for food. They need food to give them energy to grow, to reproduce, to hunt their prey, and to avoid their enemies, for most sea creatures are both hunters and hunted.

All sea animals depend on plankton. Plankton depends on the sun, as well as on a rich supply of minerals dissolved in the water. In temperate waters, when the hours of sunlight are short, many creatures go hungry as the supply of plankton runs out. The animals who cannot migrate to regions where there is more food lose weight and stop reproducing themselves.

The feeding patterns of sea animals are like a pyramid. The huge quantities of phytoplankton are at the bottom. The pyramid rises in stages to a few animals at its peak.

On land such a pyramid might show sheep eating grass and man eating sheep. But the animals of the sea are so much smaller at the base of the pyramid and so much larger at its peak that far more steps have to be taken to reach the top. At the peak are animals with no predators—unless they are preyed on by man.

The direct link from the animal at the top of the pyramid down to the plankton is called a food chain.

Plankton growth

Very few plants (colored green in the diagram) grow in winter, and only a few animals (pink) survive, mostly feeding on each other. The spring sunlight brings a plant explosion, and by summer the animal life has multiplied too. There is a second, smaller plant boom in autumn.

Minerals from the deep

The deep, cold layers of the oceans are rich in minerals because there are no plants to absorb them. Winter storms and upwellings bring them to the surface. Upwellings can happen when constant offshore winds blow the surface water. The deep water wells up to replace it. This also happens where currents diverge.

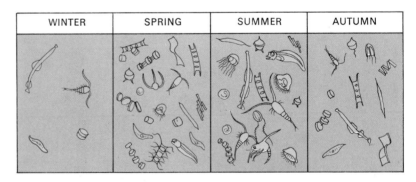

WINTER	SPRING	SUMMER	AUTUMN

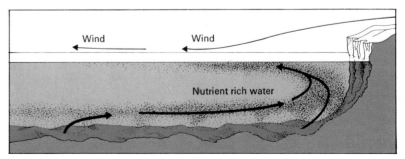

Wind   Wind

Nutrient rich water

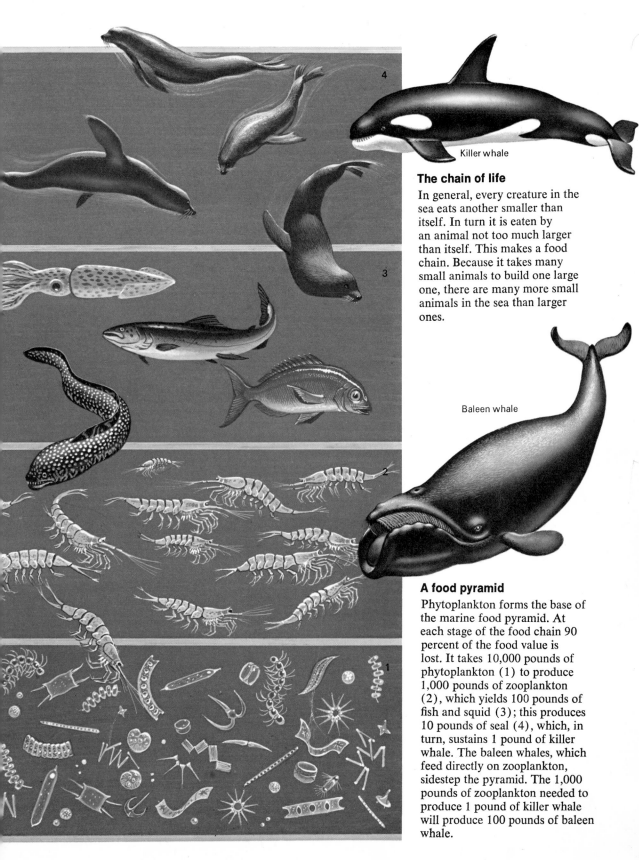

Killer whale

The chain of life

In general, every creature in the sea eats another smaller than itself. In turn it is eaten by an animal not too much larger than itself. This makes a food chain. Because it takes many small animals to build one large one, there are many more small animals in the sea than larger ones.

Baleen whale

A food pyramid

Phytoplankton forms the base of the marine food pyramid. At each stage of the food chain 90 percent of the food value is lost. It takes 10,000 pounds of phytoplankton (1) to produce 1,000 pounds of zooplankton (2), which yields 100 pounds of fish and squid (3); this produces 10 pounds of seal (4), which, in turn, sustains 1 pound of killer whale. The baleen whales, which feed directly on zooplankton, sidestep the pyramid. The 1,000 pounds of zooplankton needed to produce 1 pound of killer whale will produce 100 pounds of baleen whale.

Static animals

While free-swimming animals seek food in the open sea, 90 percent of all marine species stay in the same place all the time. They live either permanently fixed to rock or slither, creep, or crawl along the ocean floor. Most of these animals live in the relatively shallow waters of the continental shelf, where a steady rain of plankton falls from the sunlit layers above.

Some animals wave tentacles through the water to gather in fragments of food. Others pump the plankton-rich water through their bodies. Those living on the sea floor sift through the sand or mud for anything missed by those above.

As these animals cannot escape from predators by swimming away, many defend themselves with poisonous barbs or by changing colors to confuse the enemy.

Animals of the sea bed

The sea bed is really a world of the invertebrates, or animals without backbones. There are countless numbers of worms, anemones, corals, jellyfish, crabs, shrimps, and shells. A typical selection of bottom-dwelling animals (above) include: goose barnacles (1); blue starfish (2); red beard sponge (3); mussels (4); pink-hearted hydroid (5); brittle star (6); whelk (7); lugworm (8); periwinkle (9); African limpet (10); fan worms (11); crab (12); European cockle (13); sea slug (14); scallop (15); sea vase (16); sea cucumber (17); anemones (18).

Filter-feeding sponges

Sponges feed by absorbing water through tiny holes on their bodies (1). The water is filtered through tissues, the food extracted, and the water pumped out again through a hole at the top of the sponge (2).

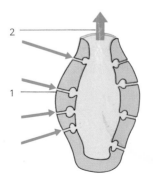

Anemones

With the poisonous barbs on its tentacles (1), a sea anemone can stun small fish and crustaceans. The prey is sucked into a bag-shaped stomach (2), where it is digested and the waste is expelled through the mouth (3).

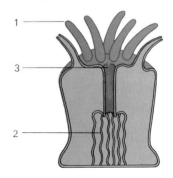

Coral

Corals are related to anemones and jellyfish. Enormous coral reefs, which provide a home for many other marine organisms, are formed from the hard skeletons of countless coral animals, or polyps. Polyps are soft, tube-shaped organisms, generally much smaller than anemones. Most coral colonies contain thousands of polyps. There are a great many kinds of coral, which grow in a variety of beautiful shapes.

Sea urchins

A sea urchin has a shell-like body protected by numerous spines (1). In between the spines are many tube feet (2) on which it moves. It has teeth (3) to eat seaweed and other smaller organisms.

Worms

There are thousands of species of worms. The bootlace worm, which can be up to 100 feet long, hides under a stone to wait for its prey. Bristle worms have jaws and can eat animals larger than themselves.

Mollusks

Mollusks include snails and octopus as well as the mussel shown here. Mussels are bivalves, or twin-shelled (1). They feed by taking water into the mouth (2), passing it over the gills where the food is extracted, and then ejecting the water (3).

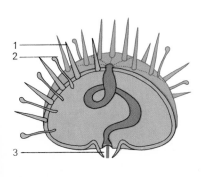

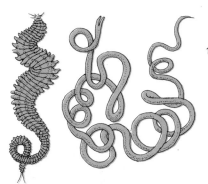

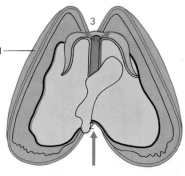

Hide and go seek

Many sea animals use camouflage to get near their prey or to escape their enemies. The most common form, used by all fast swimmers, is a bluish color on the top of the body, with silver underneath. Seen from above, the fish merges with the color of the deeper water. From below, it takes on the lighter color of the sunlit surface.

Slower swimmers often use complicated color changes. Pigment-bearing cells under their scales expand or contract so that an animal can take on the color, or even the allover pattern, of its surroundings.

Some fish are permanently disguised as weed-covered rocks or floating seaweed. Others have brightly colored patterns or markings, like an "eye" near their tail, to get a predator to strike there instead of at their head.

Besides acting as a disguise, and sometimes as a warning, bright colors and patterns help animals find their own kind for reproduction.

One way free-swimming fish protect themselves is by swimming together in a shoal, or school. Some fish spend their entire lives in the same school. Each night the school breaks up and re-forms again the next morning. If one of its members is caught by a predator, the fish scatter, coming together again after the danger has passed. Sometimes the fish all swim and turn together so evenly that the entire school is mistaken for one large animal.

An unusual kind of free-floating seaweed grows in a vast area of the Atlantic known as the Sargasso Sea. Many animals, including frog fish, pipe fish, crabs, shrimps, barnacles, and sea slugs, are specially adapted to live there. All use camouflage to blend with the weeds.

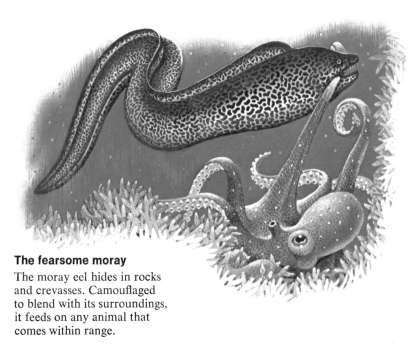

The fearsome moray

The moray eel hides in rocks and crevasses. Camouflaged to blend with its surroundings, it feeds on any animal that comes within range.

Armed with poison

The spines of the brightly colored lion fish, which lives among coral reefs, are very poisonous. The much duller scorpion fish is protected in the same way. It is probably more dangerous because it is harder to see and can surprise its prey. The cowrie shell is harmless.

Friends and protectors

Pilotfish swim with sharks—though not too close to the shark's jaws—getting protection from the larger animal and benefiting from any food it may find. Clown fish lure their predators within reach of the anemones' poison barbs while they remain sheltered among the tentacles.

Spiny defenses

The porcupine fish inflates itself by swallowing air or water so that its spines stand out. This discourages predators. The sea urchin's spines are also used for defense, but they fail with the trigger fish whose horny beak can snap the spines.

Cleaners

The tiny wrasse, only 4 inches long, will clean other fish such as the grouper to keep them free from parasites and to remove diseased flesh. Schools of fish, or even lone fish, will line up patiently at "cleaning stations" to wait for their turn. The wrasse cleans inside their mouths and even enters the tender gills of fierce predatory fish. As well as wrasse, there are a number of other cleaner fish and some cleaner shrimps.

The free swimmers

Most sea creatures move about slowly on the ocean floor, if at all. Others, like the tiny plankton, drift helplessly with the tides and currents. But the free-swimming forms of ocean life are strong enough to roam the seas in search of food. They are known as the nekton—"that which swims." The nekton includes the best-known forms of marine life: fish, mammals like the dolphins, reptiles like turtles, even birds such as the penguins. With the exception of the jet-propelled squid, all these are higher animals with backbones (vertebrates). Most are streamlined so that they can move swiftly through the waters, to find prey or to avoid being preyed on themselves.

Many of the fish of the nekton live out their entire lives in the surface waters. The pressure at greater depths could crush their bones.

The illustration shows typical fish of the warm ocean (not to scale). They range in size from the dolphin, 12 feet, and the plankton-eating sunfish, 8 feet 3 inches, to the tiny hatchetfish, 1 inch long.

1. Flying fish
2. Blue marlin
3. Sunfish
4. Dolphin
5. Bluefin tuna
6. Bonito
7. Squid
8. Opah
9. White-tipped shark
10. Pilotfish
11. Dealfish
12. Hatchetfish
13. Hatchetfish
14. Roosterfish
15. Beryx
16. Melanocetus cirrefer

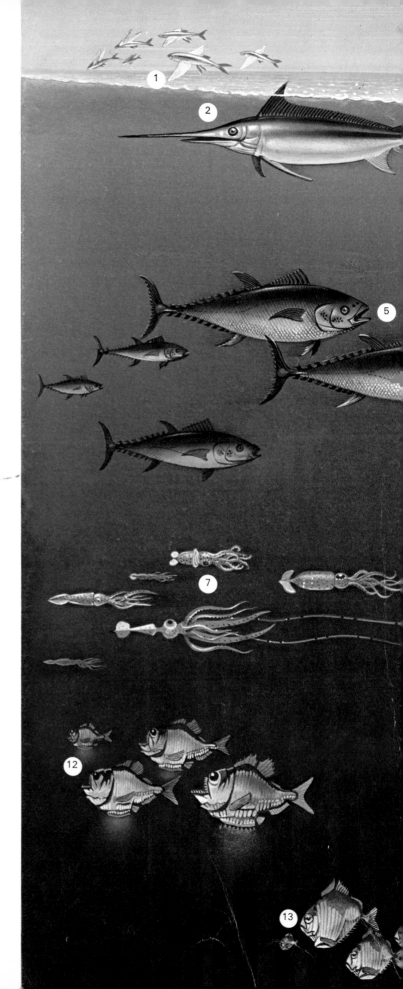

A world of darkness

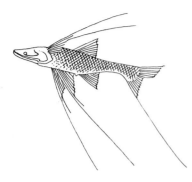

The tripod fish
The tripod fish uses three elongated fins to "walk" across the sea floor, probing for food among the ooze.

A few animals live in the chill, dark abyss. The terrible weight of the overhead waters presses down heavily on them. They are some of the strangest-looking creatures on earth.

Because it is impossible to search for food in the darkness, all the fish have huge mouths that can hold anything eatable that comes within reach—even one of their own kind. Although they all have large mouths, most of the fish are small, with little fins and transparent jellylike flesh.

The fish of the abyss have small eyes that can only just tell light from dark. To hunt for food in the darkness, the fish have "flashlights," or luminous organs, on various parts of their bodies.

The angler fish has an elongated dorsal fin that forms a "fishing line" above its upper jaw. At the end of this "line" there is a light to act as "bait" to draw its prey toward its mouth. Another species of angler has a light directly inside its mouth, to tempt a fish to swim right in, past its jaws.

Worms, crabs, and mollusks sift through the ooze of the deep-sea floor for bits of dead fish and the remains of plankton from the sunlit layers above. Jellyfish, starfish, and a variety of flatfish also live in the ooze, and some even exist in the deepest ocean chasms.

The inverse pyramid
Many fish in the abyss feed on the sinking remains of plants and animals from higher levels. Some mid-deep fish, like lantern fish, swim to the upper layers, usually at night, to collect food. The deep-sea fish in the illustration (not to scale) range in size from the 6 foot 6 inch frilled shark to the 1/5 inch angler fish.

1. Sternoptyx
2. Snipe eel
3. Rat-tail
4. Rattrap fish
5. Linophryne
6. Deep-sea prawn
7. Frilled shark
8. Gulper eel
9. Anglerfish
10. Viperfish
11. Lanternfish
12. Squid
13. Photostomias
14. Opisthoproctus
15. Lamptotoxus
16. Lasiognathus saccostoma

The squids

Squid vary in size, from a few inches long to the little-known giant squid, living in the ocean depths. Most squid are small creatures, found in the open seas. They swim by jet propulsion and sometimes reach such great speeds that they shoot out of the water.

They are powerful killers. A squid only about one foot long will kill and eat a mackerel larger than itself.

The cuttlefish, another member of the family, lives in shallow waters. It is not a fast swimmer, but it is very good at disguise. As it swims past rocks, weeds, and other objects on the sea floor, it keeps changing color to blend with its surroundings.

The octopus lives in shallow water. It hides in caves and crevasses by day, coming out at night to hunt for crabs and mollusks.

The kraken

Many sea stories tell of the kraken, a mythical creature that almost certainly owes its origins to the giant squid.

Giant squids

No one knows exactly how big the largest giant squids are. Carcasses and remains found in the stomachs of sperm whales indicate that some giant squids are longer than 55 feet, but most are probably smaller.

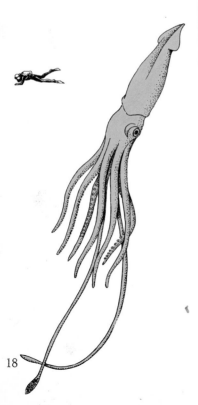

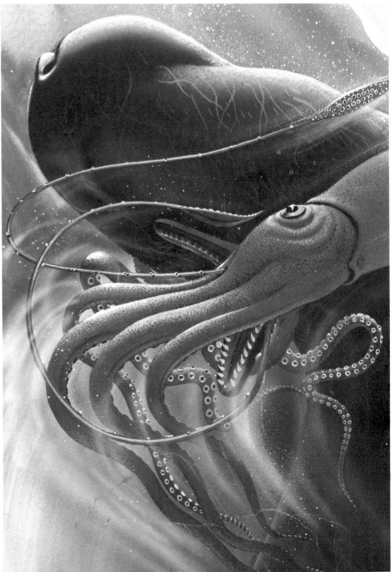

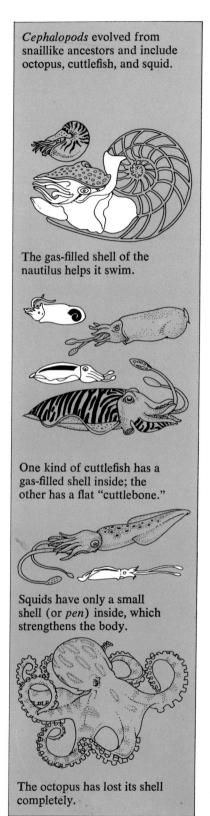

Cephalopods evolved from snaillike ancestors and include octopus, cuttlefish, and squid.

The gas-filled shell of the nautilus helps it swim.

One kind of cuttlefish has a gas-filled shell inside; the other has a flat "cuttlebone."

Squids have only a small shell (or *pen*) inside, which strengthens the body.

The octopus has lost its shell completely.

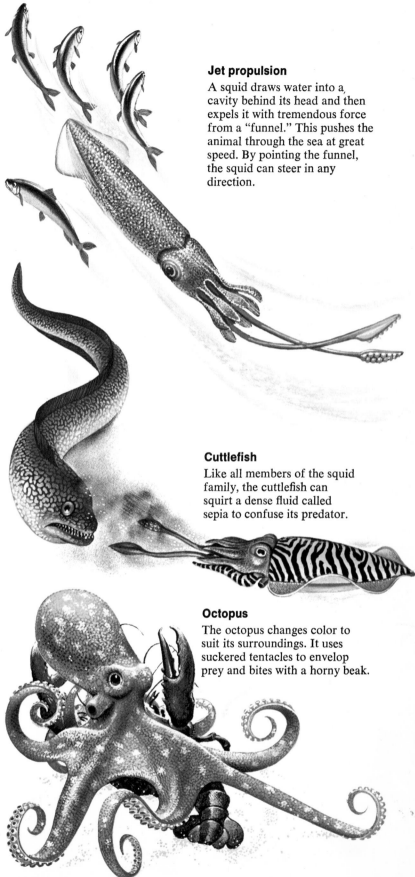

Jet propulsion

A squid draws water into a cavity behind its head and then expels it with tremendous force from a "funnel." This pushes the animal through the sea at great speed. By pointing the funnel, the squid can steer in any direction.

Cuttlefish

Like all members of the squid family, the cuttlefish can squirt a dense fluid called sepia to confuse its predator.

Octopus

The octopus changes color to suit its surroundings. It uses suckered tentacles to envelop prey and bites with a horny beak.

Sharks and rays

The earliest forms of fish had skeletons made of cartilage, a tough elastic tissue, and sharks and rays still have such skeletons. Their basic shape has stayed the same for 195 million years.

Sharks are free swimmers, found throughout the open seas. Most are scavengers as much as hunters. The largest of them, the whale sharks and basking sharks, feed only on very small organisms.

With their acute sense of smell, sharks can quickly find dead or injured fish. They will attack and swallow anything that comes within reach—cans, pieces of rope, and, occasionally, humans.

The rays live on the bottom. They have mouths on the underside of their bodies so that they can feed on shellfish from the sea bed. Some rays have a poisonous spine at the base of their tail. The largest ray, the manta, is a surface dweller, feeding on plankton.

The devilfish

The devilfish, or manta ray, can be 20 feet wide. It has a large, gaping mouth and hornlike fins rolled up on its head. It feeds on plankton, using its horns to funnel food into its mouth.

Staying afloat

A shark is heavier than water. Unless it keeps moving, it will sink. Many have livers filled with oil. Because oil is lighter than water, this helps them to stay afloat.

Teeth and jaws

Most sharks are carnivorous, or meat-eating. They have powerful jaws and sharp, serrated teeth that grow several rows deep. When the teeth in front wear down, they are replaced by those behind. Rays, which live largely on shellfish and crustacea, have flat "paving stone" teeth, which they use to crush and grind.

Skin

Sharks and rays have small, backward-pointing structures called dermal denticles rather than scales. These denticles are covered with enamellike teeth that make shark skin rough, like sandpaper. In rays the denticles are set far apart on the body and look like thorns.

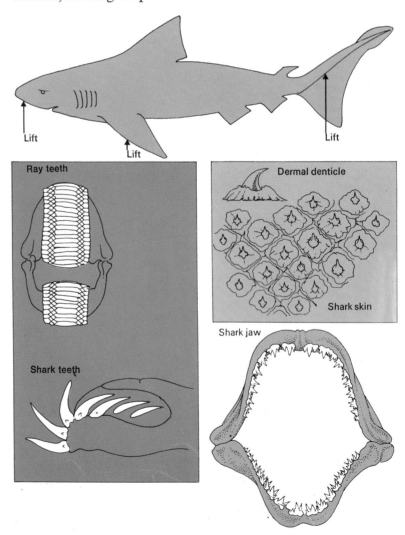

Lift

Lift

Lift

Lift

Ray teeth

Dermal denticle

Shark skin

Shark teeth

Shark jaw

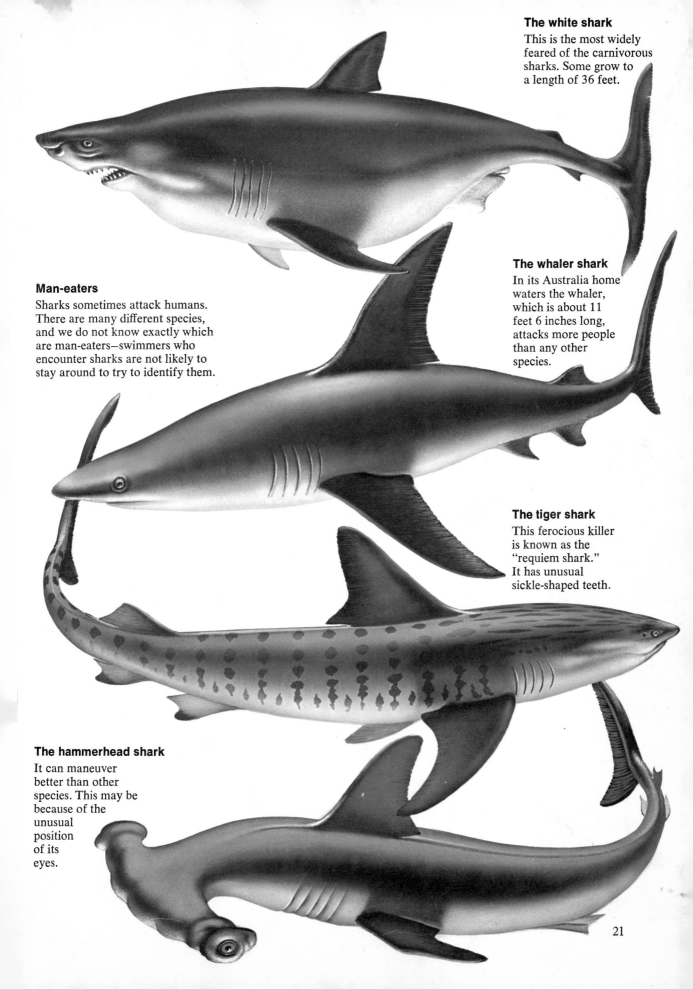

The white shark
This is the most widely feared of the carnivorous sharks. Some grow to a length of 36 feet.

Man-eaters
Sharks sometimes attack humans. There are many different species, and we do not know exactly which are man-eaters—swimmers who encounter sharks are not likely to stay around to try to identify them.

The whaler shark
In its Australia home waters the whaler, which is about 11 feet 6 inches long, attacks more people than any other species.

The tiger shark
This ferocious killer is known as the "requiem shark." It has unusual sickle-shaped teeth.

The hammerhead shark
It can maneuver better than other species. This may be because of the unusual position of its eyes.

21

Bony fish

Like other animals with hard, bony skeletons—mammals, birds, and reptiles—bony fish have a basic body plan. It can be adapted to many different shapes and sizes. As most fish are built for speed, they are usually streamlined. But some have evolved different shapes to suit a particular way of life. Sea-bed dwellers have flat, compressed bodies, with both eyes on the same side of their head.

As fish are heavier than water, many have a gas-filled swim bladder to stop them from sinking to the depths. This acts in the same way as a life jacket. The fish controls its depth by regulating the quantity of gas in the bladder. It expels gas if it wants to sink lower.

Fish are the most numerous of all species of animals with backbones, either on land or sea. There are over 20,000 species of bony fish—and all have fins, gills, and scales.

Coelacanth

Scientists thought the coelacanth became extinct 70 million years ago until living specimens were found off the East African coast in 1938. It is related to those fish that may have left the water for land life millions of years ago.

A typical fish

The bony fish are vertebrates adapted for aquatic living. They propel and balance themselves in the water with their fins, and get oxygen for breathing from the water with their gills. Most bony fish have their eyes set on either side of their head. This means that though the structure of their eyes is similar to that of a human eye, they have monocular, not binocular, vision.

Gills

Gills do the same job for fish as lungs do for mammals. They contain many thin-walled folds of skin (lamellae) with a very rich blood supply, and hang from the gill arch. There are usually four on either side of the fish. Water is taken into the mouth for respiration and passes over the gills, where oxygen is absorbed and carbon dioxide expelled. The water is then pushed out under the gill covers.

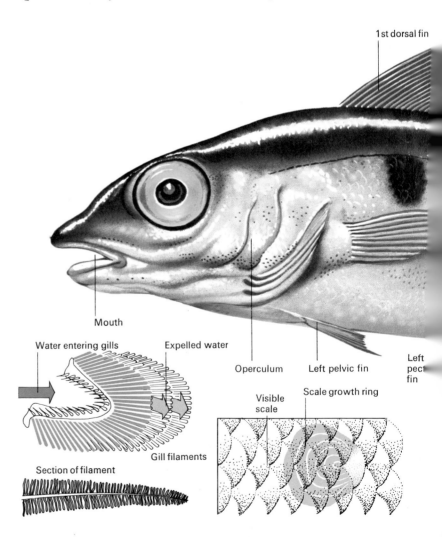

1st dorsal fin

Mouth

Water entering gills

Expelled water

Gill filaments

Section of filament

Operculum

Left pelvic fin

Visible scale

Scale growth ring

Left pect fin

22

Swimming

A typical fish has a strong but flexible back. The muscles on each side of the spine contract alternately. This results in a sideways and backward thrust against the water, pushing the fish forward.

Swimming motion

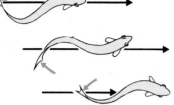

Puffer fish

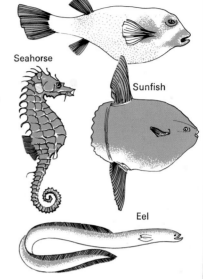

Seahorse

Sunfish

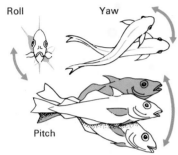

Roll

Yaw

Pitch

Eel

The use of fins

The basic flexing motion of a fish swimming is not enough to allow it to travel where it wishes. The median single fins keep it vertical in the water, preventing roll and stopping it yawing from side to side. The paired fins keep it horizontally stable, preventing pitch.

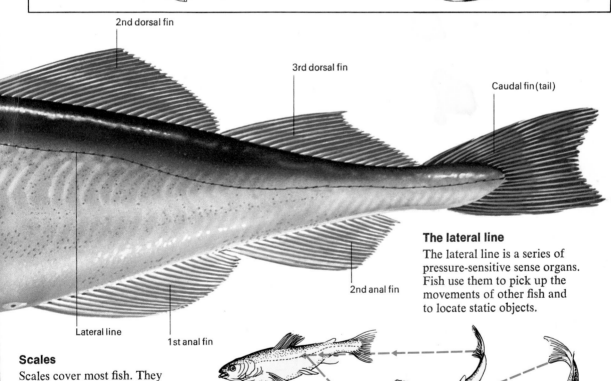

2nd dorsal fin

3rd dorsal fin

Caudal fin (tail)

The lateral line

The lateral line is a series of pressure-sensitive sense organs. Fish use them to pick up the movements of other fish and to locate static objects.

2nd anal fin

Lateral line

1st anal fin

Scales

Scales cover most fish. They protect the fish and grow with it, and growth rings can be used to determine age. The scales are covered with mucus, which cuts down friction from the water and prevents parasites from settling. Scales develop only when the fish is fully grown.

The whales

Although they are mammals, whales spend their entire lives in the ocean. They resemble fish in shape, but there are many basic differences between them.

Instead of tails, whales have horizontal flukes, which they beat up and down to drive themselves through the water. Like all mammals, they must breathe air. They do this through blowholes on the top of their heads when they rise to the surface. Whale calves are born underwater, and the cow nudges the baby to the surface so that it can take its first breath. At first the calf is nursed on the surface so that it can breathe at the same time, but later it learns to nurse underwater.

Whales do not have scales as fish do, nor sweat glands, like other mammals. They have a layer of blubber under their skin that protects them against changes in the temperature. They can also draw nourishment from this layer when food is scarce.

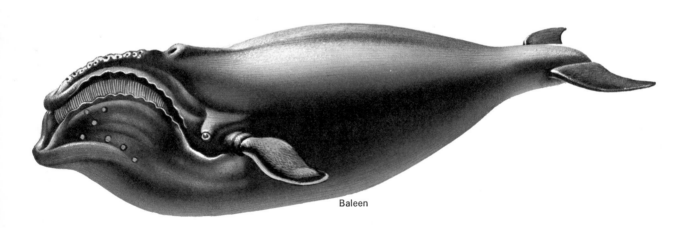

Baleen

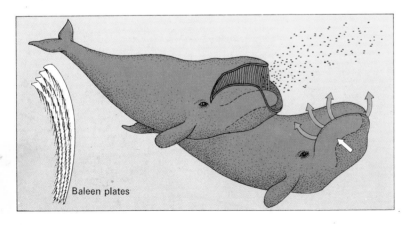

Baleen plates

Baleen whales

Baleen whales get their name from the hundreds of fringed plates, or baleen, growing from their upper jaws. Krill, a kind of shrimplike zooplankton, is sucked into the mouth together with water. This is forced out by the huge tongue, which folds back as the mouth closes, leaving the krill trapped in the baleen. The baleen whales include the largest whale—the blue whale—and the smallest whale—the sei whale.

Whales have no sense of smell. They have acute hearing and can communicate with each other underwater. They use a series of high-pitched whistles and squeaks to tell their distance from rocks, ships, or other animals. The sounds bounce off the object and the whale can tell its distance by the speed of the returning echo.

There are two kinds of whales—the whalebone, or baleen, whales and the more common toothed whales.

Measuring up to 65 feet, the sperm whale is the largest toothed whale, but it is still far smaller than the huge baleen whale. A sperm whale can dive over half a mile deep in search of giant squid, and can often stay underwater for over an hour.

The whalebone, or baleen whales, which include the giant blue whale weighing up to 150 tons, do not need to dive for their food, for they feed on zooplankton. They can swim as fast as 30 miles per hour.

Narwhal

Killer whales

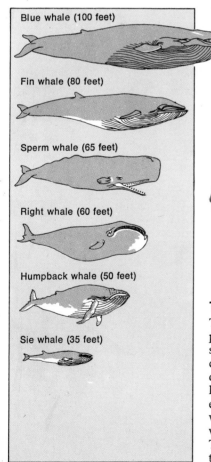

Blue whale (100 feet)

Fin whale (80 feet)

Sperm whale (65 feet)

Right whale (60 feet)

Humpback whale (50 feet)

Sie whale (35 feet)

Toothed whales
This group includes dolphins and porpoises, beaked whales and sperm whales. They usually have cone-shaped teeth and live mainly on fish and squid. Killer whales hunt in packs, and will sometimes eat seals, small whales, and walruses. The narwhal, one of the whales of the Arctic, has a tusk. This has developed from its single tooth and may grow up to 9 feet.

Other mammals

Sea otter

Sea otters live on the kelp beds off the North Pacific coasts. To prevent their being washed away on the tide while they sleep, they wrap the seaweed around themselves.

Most sea mammals still come ashore to breed, but they have become so adapted to life in the water that they are clumsy and helpless on land.

Seals are the most numerous mammals in the ocean and can swim fast enough to catch fish and squid. There are two basic kinds of seals—the eared seals, which include fur seals and sea lions, and the true seals. Both swim using their flippers and sinuous bodies. The eared seals use their forelimbs to give them thrust, while the true seals use their hind limbs. True seals can also dive deeply and stay underwater for as long as 20 minutes.

Walruses, like seals, are streamlined. They can also dive to great depths, where they find food with the help of their sensitive "mustache." Both males and females use their tusks to dig for shellfish and to haul themselves out of the water

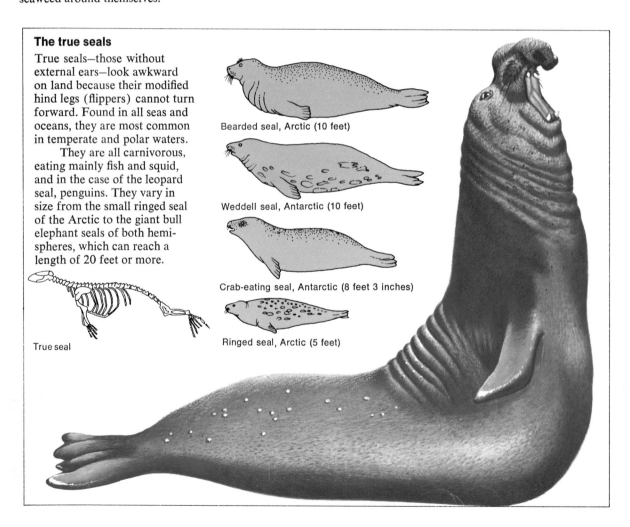

The true seals

True seals—those without external ears—look awkward on land because their modified hind legs (flippers) cannot turn forward. Found in all seas and oceans, they are most common in temperate and polar waters.

They are all carnivorous, eating mainly fish and squid, and in the case of the leopard seal, penguins. They vary in size from the small ringed seal of the Arctic to the giant bull elephant seals of both hemispheres, which can reach a length of 20 feet or more.

True seal

Bearded seal, Arctic (10 feet)

Weddell seal, Antarctic (10 feet)

Crab-eating seal, Antarctic (8 feet 3 inches)

Ringed seal, Arctic (5 feet)

onto the ice. They are now found only in the north of Greenland and the Bering Strait.

The dugongs and manatees, also called sea cows, are similar to seals and walruses in shape but are in no way related. These completely vegetarian mammals spend their entire lives in shallow coastal waters, tearing up sea plants with their bristly mustaches.

The only mammals to have retained their hind legs, in spite of spending their lives in the water, are the sea otters. They are also one of the few mammals to use a tool. They crack open clam shells against a stone, as they float on their backs in the kelp beds of the Californian or Alaskan coasts, and then use their chests as tables. They have thick underfur, which traps a layer of air to help them keep warm in the water.

The dugong
These large, slow-moving vegetarians live in shallow seas. Strange though it seems, they were once thought to be the mermaids of sailors' tales.

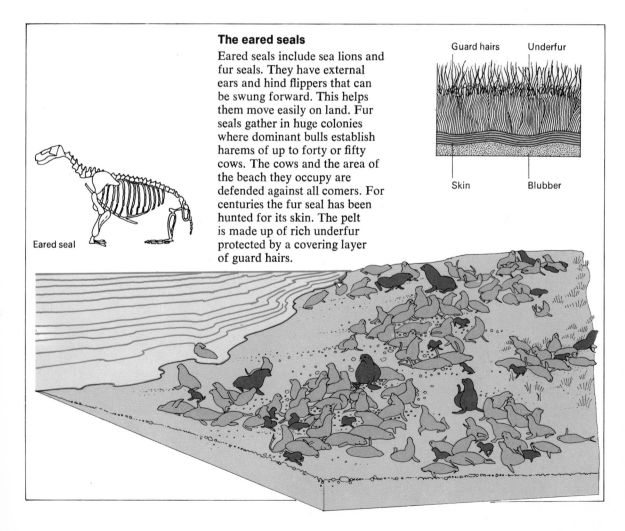

The eared seals
Eared seals include sea lions and fur seals. They have external ears and hind flippers that can be swung forward. This helps them move easily on land. Fur seals gather in huge colonies where dominant bulls establish harems of up to forty or fifty cows. The cows and the area of the beach they occupy are defended against all comers. For centuries the fur seal has been hunted for its skin. The pelt is made up of rich underfur protected by a covering layer of guard hairs.

Eared seal

Guard hairs   Underfur

Skin   Blubber

Birds and reptiles

Many sea birds, such as gulls, gannets, and cormorants, feed around the seashores. Wading birds haunt the tidelines. These birds rarely go far out to sea.

The true sea birds are the albatrosses and shearwaters. They glide endlessly on ocean breezes and come ashore only to breed.

The penguins of the southern oceans are also adapted to a seagoing life. Their wings are no longer good for flying but help them swim fast enough to compete with the larger fish, whose shape they resemble underwater. As well as being able to spend months in the water, penguins can live on land for many weeks. Emperor penguins incubate their eggs on land for 63 days. On land or sea, penguins always stay together. They build huge colonies for breeding their young, the males and females taking turns rearing the chicks and hunting for food. Their oily feathers, together with a thick

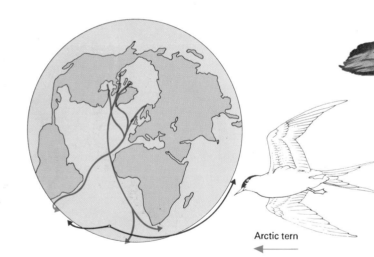

Arctic tern

Albatross

Birds of the sea

The Arctic tern migrates from the northern hemisphere to the Antarctic—22,000 miles in all. Albatrosses live out at sea and return to land only every other year to breed. Penguins of the southern oceans are totally adapted to a seagoing life. The ocean supplies all their food.

layer of blubber, make it possible for penguins to stand intense cold and long periods without food.

Two kinds of reptile have adapted to live in the sea—the turtle and the sea snake. Because they are cold-blooded, they are found only in the warmer seas.

All sea snakes are venomous and are closely related to the land-dwelling cobras. Some varieties breed only at sea, bearing their young live, and are quite helpless on land. A few other species breed on shore and lay eggs.

Turtles' front feet have become large, strong flippers and their shells have narrowed toward the back to make them more streamlined. They cannot withdraw their heads or their flippers into their shells as land turtles do. Male turtles live their entire lives at sea, but the females come ashore to breed. They remain on land only long enough to lay their eggs.

Sea snakes

Found mostly in the Indian Ocean and the Pacific, sea snakes are adapted to marine life.

Sea turtles

The female turtles make sighing noises as they plow up the beach. They dig a hole and lay about 100 eggs before returning to the sea. As soon as the young hatch, they scramble to the surface and head for the water. Predators often attack both eggs and young.

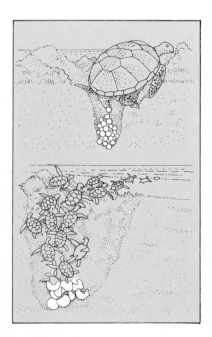

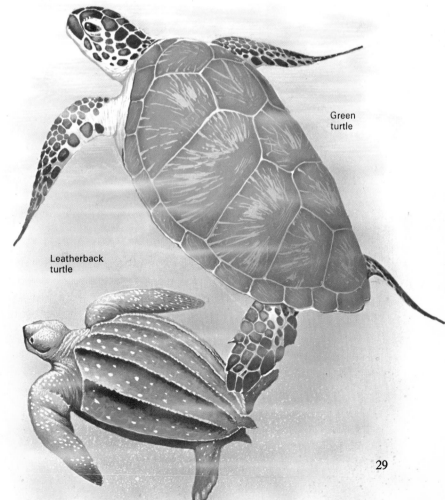

Green turtle

Leatherback turtle

Ocean giants

Dinosaurs were once the giants of the land, but became extinct millions of years ago. But there are giants in the sea today that are the largest animals ever to have existed. These are the blue whales, which can be 100 feet long and weigh 30 times as much as an African elephant—the largest land animal alive today. These whales grow so large because their enormous frames are supported by the surrounding water.

Until the arrival of man, these harmless giants had no enemies, but now they are hunted for their oil and blubber. Many whale species are in danger of extinction. For some it is already too late. Like the dinosaur, some whales may become just another museum exhibit to be marveled at.

Friends and foes

Not all ocean giants are as fierce as they look, but the killer whale, up to 30 feet long, is a savage predator, eating almost any animal large enough to attract its attention. It is dwarfed in size by the giant blue whale, the largest land or sea animal. In spite of its huge size—it weighs 150 tons and measures up to 100 feet in length—this whale feeds only on small crustaceans. The whale shark is the largest of the fish. It is usually 36 feet long, but it has been known to reach a length of 50 feet. The manta ray, or devilfish, and the octopus (each 3 to 5 feet), in spite of their scary looks and the popular stories about them, do not attack people. The ray feeds on small fish and large plankton and the octopus on small crustaceans.

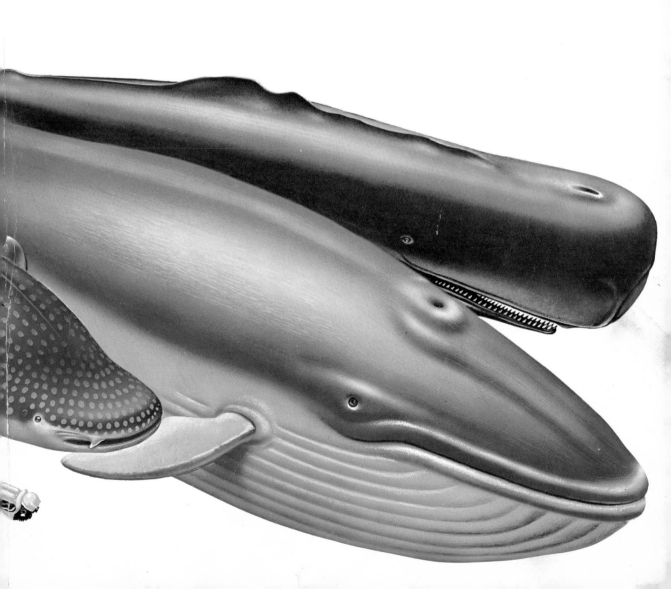